THE
BATTLEFIELD
GHOST

THE BATTLEFIELD GHOST

by Margery Cuyler

drawings by Juliana McIntyre

Thanks to: Lisa Fischetti, for reading the manuscript and commenting on the sections involving horses; John Mills, Curator and Senior Historic Preservation Specialist, the Thomas Clarke House Museum, Princeton Battlefield State Park, for assisting with the historical research; Signe Rossbach and Michael Michl for helping with the German phrases; and Mrs. Canter's fourth-grade reading class at the Campbell School in Metuchen, New Jersey, for their helpful feedback. Also thanks to George and Olivia Sowles for their input.

ISBN: 1453863400
EAN-13: 9781453863404
LCCN: 2010914996

12 11 10 9 8 7 6 5 4   1 2 3 4 5/0

Printed in the U.S.A

To Miss Doreen Griffin,
former third-grade teacher extraordinaire,
Johnson Park School, Princeton, New Jersey

CONTENTS

CHAPTER ONE

A GHOST IN THE HOUSE?

JOHN stood in the yard and gazed up at the large stone house looming above him. Green shutters hung crookedly from the windows, and some were even missing. The walls were choked with ivy, and the glass in two of the upstairs windows was cracked.

"Don't just stand there staring," said Mom as she carried a box of books into the house. "I need your help bringing in stuff from the car."

John sighed. He didn't feel like helping because he didn't feel like moving. Who wanted to live in a house that was nowhere near his school or his best friend Obadiah's? And why move into a house that was said to be haunted? But Mom and Dad didn't believe in ghosts. They had dreamed about living in this house ever since John could remember. They were both crazy about old houses, and this one was more than three hundred years old. It was even older than the Constitution and had been around during the Revolutionary War.

John's ten-year-old sister, Lisa, went running by with her parakeet, Waldo. He was gripping his perch tightly as the cage jostled back and forth.

"Want to come down to the basement?" she asked. "And help me turn it into an animal hospital? We'll call it the Lisa C. Perkins Home for Lost and Injured Pets."

"Not now, Lisa. Later, okay?"

John was more in the mood to check out the living room and see if his piano had been moved to the spot near the window.

As he climbed the porch steps, he bumped into his father coming out the front door. Mr. Perkins was carrying a huge plant.

"Mom thinks we should leave our houseplants outside until she can figure out where to put them." He swept his arm toward the field next to the house. "She's going to go nuts with all this space for a garden."

"Uh-huh." John squeezed past his father and trotted through the hallway to the living room. Boxes were scattered haphazardly across the Oriental rug. Mom's gardening posters were leaning against the freshly painted blue walls. John was glad to see his piano set up near the bay window, just where he'd hoped it would be. He opened the lid to the piano bench and pulled out some sheet music. It was Mozart's Sonata no. 1 in C, the piece he'd been working on with his teacher for the past two months. The runs were hard, but he liked the smooth, velvety way they sounded when he didn't make any mistakes.

He propped the music on the piano stand and began to play. As his fingers picked out the melody, the curtains in the open window seemed to sway to the melody. John closed his eyes, letting the familiar music carry his fingers over the keys. Then something strange happened. At the beginning of the next run, someone lightly touched the top of his left hand. It felt kind of like a butterfly kiss. John's eyes snapped open but no one was in the room. Then he heard a crackling sound and turned around. A small fire was burning in the fireplace.

How weird, thought John. *I didn't notice that when I came in.*

He stood up and walked over to the fireplace. The fire was sputtering as a pile of kindling and a little log struggled to stay lit. John moved the fire screen to the side and blew on the flames. As they hopscotched across the top of the log, Mom came into the room. Her blonde hair was pulled back into a ponytail and her clothes looked as if they had just come out of the laundry. How could Mom look so neat when the house was such a mess?

"I heard you playing and it sounded really nice," she said.

"Thanks," said John. "Hey, did you make this fire?"

"What fire?" asked Mom. Sure enough, when John looked back at the fireplace, the fire had gone out.

"There was a fire here . . ."

"Nonsense," said Mom. "We haven't had time to build any fires. Come on, we're going out for pizza. I could eat a whole one by myself, I'm so hungry. Dad and Lisa are already in the car."

John followed his mother down the porch steps, a fluttery feeling in his stomach. Had there been a real fire in the fireplace or had it been his imagination? And why had John felt someone touching his hand? He shrugged. *It all must have been my imagination,* he decided. *There was no one else in the room.*

As John got into the car, he heard the sound of faint piano music drifting through the open window by the front porch. A shiver ran up his spine as he leaned forward, trying to hear more.

Was he crazy or was someone playing the Mozart piece he had just practiced? The notes hung eerily in the night air as his dad drove down the driveway.

CHAPTER TWO

THE TOUCH OF A GHOST

THAT night, John slept in a sleeping bag since his stuff still wasn't unpacked. His father found a copy of *Treasure Island* in one of the book boxes. He settled down on the bed next to John and started reading. John began to relax as his father's voice droned on and on. When Dad finished the first chapter, he and John said prayers. Then his father gave him a hug and started to leave the room. "Your mother's helping Lisa make up her bed," he called from the door. "She'll come in to say good night in just a second."

John snuggled into his warm, down-filled sleeping bag. After a while, he heard Mom's footsteps in the hall. He decided to play a trick on her. When she came into the room, he'd pretend to be asleep. Then he'd leap up and say, "Just kidding." He closed his eyes as she walked over and sat on the bed. She put her palm on his forehead. Then she smoothed down his hair. Just as she was about to leave, he sprang up. But when he opened his eyes, she was gone.

"Mom!" he cried out.

But she wasn't there.

John wiggled out of his sleeping bag and dashed down the hall. He ran into Lisa's room. His mother was helping his sister make up the bed.

"Mom, did you just come into my room?" asked John.

Mom tucked in the corner of the blanket and stood up, rubbing her back.

"Oooh, I'm stiff," she said. "No, I didn't, but I was just about to."

"Lisa, did you come in?" John asked.

"No, I've been looking for my stuffed animals," she said.

John ran into his parents' bedroom, where his father was arranging some pillows on the bed.

"Have you come into my room since saying good night?" asked John.

"No," said Dad. "I've been in here."

John felt the blood drain from his face. If none of his family had come into his room, then who had?

John rubbed the back of his neck, the way he did when he was nervous or upset or both.

"What's the problem?" Mom asked, coming into the bedroom.

"I was lying in bed, pretending to be asleep, when someone or something felt my forehead. And earlier, when I was practicing the piano, someone touched my hand. That same someone could have started that fire I told you about. Those stories about there being a ghost in this house must be true! I can't stay here another minute. Not tonight, not ever."

"Nonsense," said Mom. "I'll move a light into your room. If you keep it on all night, you'll feel safe. And your imagination will stop playing tricks on you."

"That won't help," said John. "Let me sleep in here with you and Dad. Please!"

Mom sighed. "You do look awfully pale," she admitted, touching her hand to John's forehead.

Dad raised his eyebrows and shrugged. "Your freckles look like they're about to jump off your face," he remarked. "Okay, go get your sleeping bag."

Mom came over and gave John a hug. "You've got to stop believing those ghost stories, John. We'll be living in this house for a long time."

John looked at his mother. He thought about the cool hand he'd felt on his forehead and the music he'd heard. No matter what his mother said, he knew he'd never get used to this house. It was the creepiest place he'd ever been.

CHAPTER THREE

THE HAUNTED STALL

THE next morning, John woke up to sunlight streaming through the window of his parents' bedroom. As he watched it dancing on the carpet, he wondered if his mother was right. Maybe he had imagined the ghostly events of yesterday.

He rolled out of his sleeping bag and went down the back stairs to the kitchen. His parents were up and dressed. The coffeemaker was going and Dad was making English muffins. Dad was wearing his BAD HAIR DAY T-shirt. His wiry hair was sticking straight up in the air, the way it did when he hadn't combed it yet.

"I found our toaster just now," said Mom. "Your father went out and got juice, milk, muffins, and cereal. Wasn't that nice? Lisa's still in bed."

The kitchen was flooded with light. Lisa's two golden retrievers, Duncan and Doughnut, were asleep underneath the table. John leaned over and stroked their thick, golden fur. He sat down and let the sunshine streaming through the window seep into his bones.

After breakfast, John felt much better. The events of the day before seemed like a bad dream. He felt as if he could go back to his room and start unpacking.

The movers had set up his desk and bunk beds, but there was still a lot to do. He opened a few boxes, searching for his music posters and CDs. Before they'd moved, he'd been working on a story about a dog that ate a magic dog biscuit and turned into an alien. If he could find his computer, he could finish the story before school started in two weeks.

While he was moving a box of school supplies over to his desk, the phone rang.

"John," Dad called. "It's Obadiah."

"Hey, man," said Obadiah when John picked up the phone. "What's happening? Have you seen any old ghosts in that haunted house of yours?"

"No ghosts yet," said John. He bit his lip, hoping Obadiah would change the subject.

"You wait," said his friend. "My aunt Rose says that there was a black woman staying in your house a long time ago who got chased down the driveway by a soldier ghost."

"I don't believe it," said John. "You're exaggerating, as usual."

"It's true!" said Obadiah. "My aunt Rose never lies. You'd better be careful."

"Thanks, pal. If I see a soldier walking around the house, I'll let you know."

"Hey, can you come over?"

"Can't," said John. "I have too much to do."

"Okay," said Obadiah. "See you."

John hung up the phone and went into Lisa's room. She was changing the floor covering in her parakeet Waldo's cage. Her bird was chirping happily on his perch. He must be getting used to his new home, John decided. Lisa's cats, Nikki and Boomerang, were curled up on a blanket on top of the radiator.

"I wish you'd come with me to the basement," Lisa remarked. "I need help fixing it up. After I wash the windows, it will be nice. There's a sink and loads of shelves."

"I'd rather go outside," said John, "and explore the barn."

"Okay," said Lisa. "That sounds like fun. Let's go after lunch."

That afternoon, after unpacking all morning, they stepped over the boxes scattered in the hallway and went out to the barn. It smelled of mildew, musty hay, and mud. It had a small first story, with horse stalls on either side of a wide corridor. There were doors on the ends of the building big enough for a wagon to fit through. "In the olden days, farmers probably drove their horses in one side and out the other," said Lisa.

They went up to the loft and poked around, but all they found was a bunch of hay.

"This must be where they stored things," said John. "We could keep a lot of stuff here, too. Like our Ping-Pong table."

"And our dartboard," added Lisa. "Let's go look at the stalls. Mom and Dad might get me a horse. They have no excuse now that we have a barn and some space. Besides, I'm old enough to take care of one. After three years of lessons at the McDonnells' farm, I know what I'm doing."

They climbed down the ladder. A well-worn bridle and reins hung from a hook on one of the walls.

Lisa went over to the first stall and ran her hand along the door. Suddenly, she stumbled forward, as if someone had pushed her.

"What's wrong?" asked John.

Again Lisa reached out to touch the wood and again she stumbled forward.

"Someone just shoved me!"

"Lisa," whispered John. "I didn't tell you this before, but yesterday, when I was practicing the piano, I felt someone touch my hand. It was such a gentle touch, though, I wasn't sure."

Lisa's eyes grew big. "Do you think it was a ghost? Maybe all those stories are true. I bet this place *is* haunted." She spun around. "I'm getting out of here!" She ran outside.

John turned to follow, but as he did, he felt something lightly grip his arm. Someone or something invisible was pushing him toward the stall. He wanted to run, but his feet felt like lead, the way they did in a nightmare if something scary was chasing him and he couldn't move. When he was only a few inches from the stall door, the invisible hand let go. Then a strange calmness washed over him. He had the feeling that the ghost—or whatever it was—would not harm him. He sensed it was trying to tell him something. He waited for a few minutes, but nothing more happened.

John could hear Mom, Dad, and Lisa walking from the house.

"I've never heard of such a thing," said Mom. "A ghost who goes around touching people! We've only been in this house for twenty-four hours, and already you and John are telling us

stories about a ghost. Your father and I haven't
seen or felt anything."

"I know I felt something," said Lisa. "Hurry.
John's still in there."

John ran to the barn door to meet them.

"Are you all right?" asked Dad, looking around
quickly and adjusting his glasses.

"I think so," said John. "But I did feel something.
Whatever it was, it's gone now."

Dad took Mom's hand and they walked over to
the horse stalls. They stood for a moment. "I don't
feel anything," Dad said, and he started to laugh
nervously. "You guys really frightened me for
a minute. Come on, let's go back to the house.
There are no ghosts here."

But Mom hesitated. "There is kind of a strange
feeling in this barn," she said. She put her arms
around Lisa and John. "But you can't really believe
that a ghost pushed you." She paused. "Maybe you
just lost your balance on this uneven floor. Let's
go roast some marshmallows and forget about this
whole thing."

As they left the barn, John caught Lisa's eye. Her skin was chalky white. No matter what Mom and Dad said, he could tell that she, too, knew something very strange had just happened.

John looked at the field that stretched beyond the barn. The purple shadows of late afternoon spread across the mud and stubble. The sky was a deep pink, the trees etched against it like dark skeletons. He looked over his shoulder. John wasn't sure, but he thought he saw the door to the barn swing back and forth. Had the ghost moved it or was it just the wind?

CHAPTER FOUR

"I WISH HE'D GO AWAY"

AFTER dinner, John followed Lisa to the basement. She had made an obstacle course out of packing boxes for her tarantula, Cuddles. The spider was scuttling back and forth, trying to find a way out.

John sat down on the floor, hugging his knees. "We need to talk," he said.

Lisa picked up Cuddles and put him on her arm. "I don't like that ghost," she commented. Cuddles paraded up her arm to investigate the sleeve of her T-shirt.

"I didn't either, at first," said John. "But listen to this. Last night, when I was trying to go to sleep, I felt something invisible touch my forehead. That's why I slept in Mom and Dad's room. And today, after you ran out of the barn, I felt something invisible grip my arm. I wasn't exactly pushed, though. It was almost as if I were being guided to the first stall. I got the feeling the ghost was trying to tell me something."

"That's scary," said Lisa. "I wish he'd go away. It's creepy to feel someone invisible touch you. What if next time he puts his hands around my neck?" She shuddered as she stroked Cuddles, who had reached her shoulder.

"I don't think the ghost is dangerous. When he was in my room last night, he was gentle. That's why I thought it was Mom putting me to bed. I have to find out more. I'm going to the library tomorrow to get a book on ghosts. Maybe I'll learn something that will help."

"What will Mom and Dad say when they find out you're doing that?"

"I won't tell them. You know they don't like hearing about the ghost. Besides, he didn't

touch them, he touched us. He's trying to tell *us* something. I just know it."

"Maybe you're right," said Lisa. "But if he touches me again, I'll start kicking him!"

She stuck out her hand and Cuddles climbed on top, exploring the hairs on her skin. "I wish Cuddles would have babies," she said. "Then I could sell one to you for fifty dollars."

But baby tarantulas were the last thing on John's mind. And who wanted to spend fifty dollars on a hairy baby tarantula, anyway?

The next day, John went to the library and checked out a book called *Ghosts and Spirits.* He learned that some people believe ghosts haunt places where, as humans, they died before solving some important problem. Their spirits roam restlessly until the problem gets solved. Sometimes humans try to communicate with them. The book described a group of people tipping a table back and forth to send signals to spirits in the other world. John quickly closed the book. He wasn't quite ready to do that.

John went back to the barn several times that week, hoping for more contact with the ghost. But nothing happened. When he stood by the stall where the ghost had been, he didn't feel any pressure on his arm at all.

And now it was time for school to start. Mom took John and Lisa to the store to get new clothes. She also bought them backpacks and new school supplies. Before they knew it, they were standing outside on the street, waiting for the school bus to pick them up.

CHAPTER FIVE

SOLDIER GHOST

JOHN was in Ms. Griffin's fourth-grade class. She was the oldest teacher in the school, yet she wore the coolest clothes. She had a pair of running shoes with lime-green soles and a dachshund named Daisy that she sometimes brought to school.

Obadiah was John's deskmate. As usual, he had plenty to say. On the first day of school, Obadiah told John, "Ms. Griffin has a gold tooth in her mouth that's worth a million dollars."

"I don't believe you," said John. "No one has that much money in their mouth."

"It's true," said Obadiah. "Gold teeth are worth a fortune. My aunt Rose's new husband told me, and he knows, since he's a dentist in New York City."

"But one million dollars?" asked John.

"Yep," said Obadiah. "And there's something else about Ms. Griffin. She has a silver sports car."

"Where'd you hear that?" asked John.

"Her mechanic, George, told my mom. He said she takes it out on the highway and drives a hundred miles per hour."

"That's awesome!"

"I know," said Obadiah. "She's one cool old lady."

But the best part about Ms. Griffin was her passion for field trips. One night, the parents agreed to let the kids meet her after dinner in the soccer field behind the school. In her red gloves, Ms. Griffin pointed out the constellations: Orion, Cassiopeia, the Big Dipper. She told the class the story behind each one. The sky came alive with gods and goddesses — hunting, stealing, falling in love, and going into battle.

Later in the fall, Ms. Griffin taught a unit on the Revolutionary War. One morning, she took the class to the field across the road from the back of John's house.

"This is one of the battlefields from the war where American soldiers sacrificed their lives for the birth of a new nation," she said dramatically. In her green-soled running shoes, she marched the children up a hill and took a small American flag from her knapsack. Waving it up and down, Ms. Griffin continued, "Five thousand American troops walked ten miles from Trenton to Princeton in the middle of the night. They wrapped the wheels of their cannons and supply wagons in rags so as not to make any noise. Many of their horses were unshod and slipped on the icy road. This made the journey slow and difficult. When the soldiers stopped along the way, a few fell asleep standing up. That's how tired they were. The army was going to attack the British brigade that was stationed in Princeton. It was January third, seventeen seventy-seven, and very cold."

"How cold?" asked Carlos. Carlos had just moved from Texas to Princeton and wasn't used to cold weather.

"Very, very cold," answered Ms. Griffin. "There was snow on the ground and the troops were tattered and hungry. Some of the soldiers had no coats or proper boots. Suddenly, as they approached the brook near this field, they met a battalion of British troops coming from the other direction."

"What were the British doing awake in the middle of the night?" asked Obadiah.

"It was actually early morning by this time. The Americans had been marching all night. The British had gotten up early and were on their way to join other British troops near the Delaware River. They had been quartered at Princeton University, which in those days was called the College of New Jersey. Some had even stayed in private homes. They were just as surprised to see the American army as the American army was to see them."

John's ears perked up. Hadn't his house been a private home during the Revolutionary War? He raised his hand.

"Yes, John," said Ms. Griffin. She took out a handkerchief and blew her nose.

"My family just moved into the old farmhouse across the street. Do you think it was used by the British?"

"I'm sure it was," said Ms. Griffin. "Some people say that Hessian soldiers stayed in your house."

"What are Hessians?" asked Amanda.

"The Hessians were German soldiers that the British hired to help fight the Americans," said Ms. Griffin.

Obadiah grabbed John's arm. "See? My aunt Rose was right! You do have a soldier ghost in your house, John. It's probably a Hessian soldier ghost. How cool."

John felt a rush of excitement. Maybe his ghost really was a Hessian soldier. Maybe he had even died during the battle.

"You mean the British actually paid people from other countries to help them fight?" asked Amanda.

"Yes," said Ms. Griffin. "It was a common practice. The British didn't have enough men to work in their overseas posts and also fight the colonists in America, so they hired the Germans to help them out. The Hessian soldiers had been well trained in Germany."

John wondered if Ms. Griffin knew anything about the ghost in his house.

"Have you heard any stories about our house being haunted?" he asked.

"Well, come to think of it, I do remember an old legend about a Hessian soldier. People used to say that every year he appeared just after midnight on January third, the anniversary of the Battle of Princeton. He'd walk through the house in his uniform, but no one knows why. There are all kinds of explanations. Some people think he may have died out in the barn from a chest wound. There was a black woman in the eighteen-hundreds who claimed that on the morning of the battle's anniversary, she saw him lying in the hay in one of the stalls in the barn. He stood up, blood dripping from a wound in his chest, and chased her down the driveway!"

"I knew it! I knew it!" said Obadiah. "That's like the story Aunt Rose told me."

Usually, John believed only about half of what Obadiah said. But this time, it looked like Obadiah was right. The Perkins' new house really was haunted. And probably by a Hessian soldier ghost at that.

Ms. Griffin put her flag back in her knapsack. "I think we've heard enough about ghosts today. Let's walk up the driveway and visit the Thomas Clarke House. Wounded soldiers from both sides were carried there during the battle. General Mercer on the American side was said to have died from bayonet wounds in one of the bedrooms days after the battle. Many Americans and British died. Our men were very courageous considering they were not as well trained or as well equipped as the enemy."

"I read somewhere that the Americans drank gunpowder mixed with rum to give them strength and courage before going into a battle!" said Obadiah.

"Yes, I read that, too," said Ms. Griffin.

For the rest of the field trip, John had a hard time concentrating. All he could think about was the Hessian ghost. He couldn't wait to get home and tell Lisa about his latest discovery.

After school, instead of practicing the piano, he went to look for his sister. He found her in the kitchen feeding the dogs. But before he could tell her what he'd learned about the ghost, she had some news for him.

"Guess what!" she said.

"What?" asked John, pouring himself a glass of orange juice.

"Mr. McDonnell—you know, the guy who teaches me riding—is going to Ireland for six months. He asked Mom and Dad if we'd like to board Arab while he's gone. They agreed, since they know how much I love that horse. I'm so excited!"

"That *is* good news," said John. "When's he coming?"

"Next weekend," said Lisa. "Will you help me clean out the barn? I have to get a stall ready, but I don't want to go back to the barn alone. Not after that ghost incident."

John took a deep breath and set his glass on the table.

"I learned more about him today," he said. "When we were on our field trip, Ms. Griffin told us that our house was used by German soldiers during the Revolutionary War. They were called Hessians and were hired by the British to fight the Americans. There's even a legend that our ghost is a Hessian soldier who appears right after midnight on the anniversary of the Battle of Princeton. He walks through the house in his uniform."

"Oh, great!" Lisa rolled her eyes.

John was going to tell her about the woman who saw the ghost lying in the hay, but then decided not to. Lisa would never go out to the barn if she heard that.

"I'm sure the ghost is trying to tell us something," said John. "I don't think he's trying to hurt us."

"Maybe so," said Lisa. "But right now, I wish he'd just go back to Germany."

"Well, I don't think he's going to go anywhere until we find out why he's haunting this house."

But there was nothing more to find out . . . until the day Arab came.

CHAPTER SIX

Arab Arrives

On Saturday, John and Lisa went out to the barn with a bucket, a mop, and a broom.

"You can clean the haunted stall," said Lisa.

"Oh, all right," grumbled John. He took the broom from Lisa. As he started sweeping, he heard a humming sound. He looked around and the humming stopped. John shrugged. Then he swept out the rest of the stall and helped Lisa lay down some fresh straw. They washed down the walls of Arab's stall. Next they straightened up the tack room, where Lisa had stored her riding equipment and some feed for Arab.

"Do you sense the ghost anywhere?" asked John. "I could swear I heard him humming!"

"Really?" said Lisa. "A musical ghost?"

Suddenly, the expression on her face changed. "Oh, no, not again. Someone is pushing me! Oh, John, do something!"

A few seconds later, John also felt a push. He and his sister were being steered toward the haunted stall. The skin on his back prickled, but then the pushing stopped, and John began to relax. He looked over at Lisa.

She had her hand on her chest, trying to steady her breathing.

Now John was more curious than ever about the ghost.

"What do you think happened in this stall?" he asked. "Do you think our Hessian had a horse that was killed here? Or perhaps this is where he died himself," he mused. He was thinking about the black woman's story. "This ghost business sure is confusing. I wish he could just tell us what he wants."

"Creepy is more like it," said Lisa. "Do we have to deal with this every time we come out to the barn? Which will be at least twice a day, once Arab arrives."

"Maybe Arab could help us solve the mystery," said John.

"Oh, sure," said Lisa. "Horses are so good at detective work."

"No, I mean it," said John. "How many kids have the chance to solve a ghost mystery? I think Arab might help us. What if the ghost touches him also?"

"And what would we learn from that?" said Lisa. "That the ghost likes horses? If that's the case, we should leave him a copy of *Black Beauty.*"

John rolled his eyes to the ceiling. Why did Lisa have to be so sarcastic?

"Stop making fun," he said.

"Oh, all right. I'll try to be brave. Let's see what happens when Arab comes."

The next morning, John and Lisa stood in the driveway, the welcoming committee for Arab the horse. Mr. McDonnell drove up to the house in his old pickup truck, towing a trailer behind him.

He parked in the middle of the driveway.

"Good morning," he said. "Arab's in fine shape today. I think he's looking forward to having a change of scene."

Mr. McDonnell had a red ponytail and was wearing a leather jacket and cowboy boots. He led Arab down the ramp of the trailer and across the yard.

In the morning sun, Arab's coat gleamed like polished wood.

Lisa took the lead rope. "John and I will take him to the barn," she offered. "His new home is all ready for him."

"Great!" said Mr. McDonnell. "I'll have some coffee with your folks, and then I'll come out and see how he's doing."

John followed his sister and Arab while Mr. McDonnell went inside the house. Lisa gave the horse some apple slices as she led him across the yard. When they got near the door, it began to bang, as if the wind were blowing it open and shut. Then John felt the familiar pressure on his arm. Arab reared up and whinnied. Lisa cried out, "There it is again. The touch of the ghost."

Arab's eyes rolled back and forth in his head. He was pawing the ground nervously.

"Do you think he sees something?" cried John.

"Yes!" yelled Lisa. "And I feel something pushing me."

John, too, was being pushed through the door. Arab was whinnying even more and jumping to the side.

Mr. McDonnell came running out of the house.

"What's wrong?" he yelled, grabbing the lead rope from Lisa and trying to calm the horse. It took a long time to settle Arab down. Finally, Mr. McDonnell was able to lead him to the stalls. As he passed the haunted stall, Arab started bucking sideways. He wouldn't go past it.

"He's sure fussy this morning," said Mr. McDonnell.

Lisa looked over at John. Her lower lip was trembling. "You were right, John," Lisa whispered. "Arab senses the ghost, too."

John put his finger to his lips. "Shhh, we don't want Mr. McDonnell to hear us talking about this."

"There, boy," said Mr. McDonnell, tugging gently on Arab's bridle until he got him into his stall. He fed the horse a lump of sugar and stroked his neck. Then he fetched a bucket of oats from the tack room and closed the gate to the stall. Arab leaned over and ate the oats hungrily.

"He'll get used to it here soon enough," said Mr. McDonnell. He patted John on the shoulder. "You and Lisa have done a nice job cleaning up the barn. Now that everything's calm, I'll go back and finish my coffee."

John wanted to believe Mr. McDonnell's words. But he wasn't sure Arab would ever get used to his new home.

Not with a ghost haunting the barn.

CHAPTER SEVEN

Fed by a Ghost

As soon as the children were alone, John said, "I wonder where the ghost is now."

Lisa put her hand to her mouth. "John, look. There are some carrots lying in the straw of the haunted stall. How did they get there? I left them in the tack room this morning."

"Mr. McDonnell probably put them there."

"I don't think so," said Lisa. "The only thing I saw him take from the tack room was the bucket of oats."

John's palms felt clammy as he looked over at his sister. She looked worried, but after a few seconds she started to smile, a half-smile that made her mouth crooked.

"Hey, I bet the ghost brought them here as a welcome present for Arab. Or maybe the ghost just likes carrots. Was he planning to eat them for lunch?"

"What if he's a vegetarian?" asked John.

Lisa chuckled and took the currycomb from the hook near the stall. She started to brush Arab's neck. "Maybe our ghost's not such a scary guy after all."

John felt hopeful as he watched his sister grooming the horse. She no longer seemed so frightened. Maybe now she'd be more interested in why the ghost was haunting the house.

"What do you think he'll do next?" asked John.

"Let's hope he'll move some bags of oats in here," said Lisa. "Or the horse blanket. He might need it to keep warm. If ghosts feel the cold, that is!"

John looked over at the carrots. Was it his imagination or were they rising up in the air? He grabbed Lisa's arm. "Look!"

Lisa leapt back.

Sure enough, the carrots were rising off the ground and floating from the haunted stall, across the aisle, into Arab's stall. The horse backed

against the wall and jerked his head up. Then he
lunged for them, pulling them delicately from an
invisible hand.

"This is great!" exclaimed John, grinning.
"Maybe the ghost will feed and groom Arab so
that you'll be free to ride him. No work and all
play!"

"Do you think?" said Lisa. "But what if the
ghost wants to ride him, too?" Worry lines
puckered her forehead.

John shrugged. "Anything could happen," he
said.

"Well," sighed Lisa, "I think I'm beginning to
agree with you. Our ghost is harmless, and he
seems to be fond of horses."

John and Lisa stood quietly and watched Arab
finish the carrots. They waited to see if anything
else would happen, but nothing did.

"I guess he went away again," said Lisa.

"I guess so," said John.

Now he really had something exciting to share
with Obadiah. As soon as Mr. McDonnell left, he
ran to the phone and dialed Obadiah's number.

"Hello?" said Obadiah.

"You wouldn't believe what just happened. The ghost turned up in the barn and fed carrots to Lisa's horse!"

"What are you talking about?"

"We saw these carrots flying through the air. They stopped in front of Arab, and I swear he started eating them."

"Arab who?"

"The horse Lisa rides over at the McDonnells' farm. We're boarding him while Mr. McDonnell is in Ireland."

"You expect me to believe your ghost was feeding carrots to some horse? Stop messing with my head!"

John chuckled. It was fun having a story to tell Obadiah for a change.

"No, really. You can ask Lisa. Those carrots flew through the air and the horse ate them!"

"I'm coming right over," said Obadiah.

But when he arrived and followed John out to the barn, there was no sign of the ghost.

"I knew you were kidding," said Obadiah.

"I wasn't," said John. "The ghost was definitely here. I promise if he shows up again, I'll call you right away."

But it wasn't until a week before Christmas that the ghost came back.

CHAPTER EIGHT

THE GHOST HORSE

A few weeks later, Dad had asked John and Lisa to help him cut down a Christmas tree in the back field.

"I'll ride Arab over and meet you there," Lisa told her father. "Arab could use some exercise."

"Could I ride with you?" asked John. "I have nothing else to do."

"Okay," said Lisa. "Let's ride bareback."

As they walked to the barn, John said, "Have you had any more visits from the ghost? Ever since you've made friends with him, I've noticed you going to the barn."

"He hasn't come back," said Lisa. "Maybe he's gone to visit his relatives in Germany for the Christmas holidays." She laughed.

"It's weird the way he comes and goes," said John. "I wonder if we'll ever learn more about him."

"He's certainly not in a hurry to give us clues," said Lisa. "Which is fine with me. Although I was hoping he'd help me out in the barn. You know, groom Arab once in a while."

As they went inside, Arab was pacing back and forth in his stall.

"He knows we're going to take him out," said Lisa.

"It's cold today," said John. "I hope Dad doesn't examine every tree in the field."

Lisa lifted the bridle off the hook and slipped it over Arab's head. She led the horse out of his stall and into the field outside. "Come on," she said to John. "Climb up behind me."

It took John three tries to hoist himself up.

"Klutz!" teased Lisa.

"Let's go," said John.

He put his hand on Arab's rump to steady himself. Lisa gently kicked the horse's sides, steering him to the path that bordered the fields behind the house.

Sunlight filtered through the branches of the trees, making patterns on the wintry grass. The children's breath left puffs of smoke in the cold air. Arab walked along rhythmically, his hooves sounding hollow on the packed dirt.

As they crossed into the next field, Arab suddenly stopped, throwing John against Lisa's back.

"That's strange," said Lisa. "I didn't make him do that."

She prodded him with her heels and he started walking again. As he moved forward, he picked up speed and began trotting toward the fence. Lisa pulled on the reins, trying to make him stop, but he kept going. John clutched his sister's shoulders.

"What's wrong?" he asked.

"I think he sees something over by the road!" yelled Lisa. "I can't seem to control him."

Arab broke into a gallop and headed straight for the road. When he reached the fence, he stopped short and perked up his ears. The children held tightly to Arab's mane as he lifted his head and whinnied. A high-pitched whinny echoed from the field across the road. Again and again Arab whinnied, and again and again a horse answered, his whinnies sounding closer and closer. But even though the children could hear the phantom horse, they couldn't see him. Lisa slipped off Arab's back and grabbed his reins. Her straight brown hair blew like a sheet around her face. "There's no real horse over there," she said. "What we're hearing is" — she paused as the words fell from her lips — "a ghost horse."

John gasped. The whinnying stopped. After a moment, Arab leaned over and began nibbling some grass.

Lisa gazed up at John, her freckles fading into the red color of her cheeks. "Our Hessian may be in Germany," she whispered, "but now another ghost has come to visit. A ghost horse."

"Do you think he has something to do with our ghost?" asked John. His heart was banging in his chest.

"Now I'm scared again," said Lisa. "What if I'm out riding and Arab tries to jump over the fence?"

"Or the ghost horse comes to visit Arab. All we need is another ghost out in the barn."

"I think we have to try again to tell Mom and Dad about what's going on. Maybe this time they'll be more sympathetic."

"I doubt they've changed," said John. He paused for a moment. "I have a better idea."

It was an idea that had been growing inside him ever since Arab had arrived. But each time it had popped into his head, John had tried to forget it. It was almost too scary to think about, much less share with his sister. But now he decided he should mention it.

"According to the legend Ms. Griffin told us," said John, "the ghost appears just after midnight on January third, the anniversary of the Battle of Princeton. If that's true, we should wait up for him and ask him to explain what's going on. Maybe he'll tell us what happened out in the barn and also what he knows about the ghost horse, if anything."

Lisa shivered. "It's one thing to get used to an invisible ghost and quite another thing to meet him."

"But talking to the ghost is the only way we'll solve the mystery. Maybe then he won't have to haunt the house any longer."

"What if he only speaks German?" said Lisa. "After all, he is a Hessian soldier."

"He could have picked up some English from being around Americans for two hundred years. . . . So, will you come?"

"I guess so," said Lisa. "I'd like to settle this ghost business once and for all."

"Great!" said John. "I didn't really want to talk to him alone."

"Let's go meet Dad," said Lisa, "and forget about ghosts between now and"— she took a deep breath—"January third."

CHAPTER NINE

CHRISTMAS

DAD was waiting for them by a large spruce. He had a big grin on his face.

"What do you think?" he asked.

"It looks too big for our living room," said John, "but it is beautiful."

"I'll trim off the lower part of the trunk," said Dad. He turned the tree on its side. "Hold it steady while I saw."

The needles pricked John's wrists as he grabbed the middle of the trunk with his mittened hands.

Lisa took a thermos from Dad's knapsack and poured herself a cup of hot chocolate.

"Yum," she said. "Here, have some." She passed the cup to John.

"Let's take this home and start decorating it," said Dad when he'd finished sawing.

Dad loaded the tree in the truck and drove back to the house. The kids followed on Arab. They left him to run in the field and went inside. Mom had brought all the Christmas boxes down from the attic. She had been collecting ornaments for years—tiny angels, soldiers with drums, red-felt Santas the kids had made, and miniature brass instruments.

John selected his favorite Christmas music, *Bach's Christmas Oratorio*. He lay down on the rug, closed his eyes, and listened to the music. In between movements, he waited to see if there was any ghostly humming in the background, but nothing happened. "I guess he's not much of a Bach fan," John thought to himself. After lunch, John would help his family decorate the tree and later, Lisa, Obadiah, and he would make holiday cookies. On the day before Christmas, their grandparents would come. Ghosts or no ghosts, Christmas this year would be the best ever.

While John stood by the hall window on December 24, watching for his grandparents to arrive, Obadiah called.

"Hey, man," he said. "Did you hear about the star on top of the Christmas tree? The one on Main Street? It got stolen!"

"No way," said John. "Who would do a weird thing like that?"

"Wait till I tell you," said Obadiah. "My aunt Rose heard that it was Amanda's older brother! The one who's in high school."

"Wow," said John. "How could he do that? He's too short to reach the top. He's not much bigger than Amanda."

"She says he used a ladder. But I bet aliens took it. How could anyone drag a ladder through all that snow?"

"Aliens?" said John. "You're crazy. Amanda must be embarrassed."

"No, but I think her brother is."

Just then, John heard a car door bang.

"Got to go," he said. "My grandparents just arrived."

"See ya," said Obadiah. "Call me later."

John ran down to the driveway. Lisa was already there, greeting Grandma and Grandpa as they got out of the car. They had driven all the way from Vermont with their three cats. When John pulled open the car door so Grandma could get out, the cats zoomed between her legs and streaked toward the field out back. Lisa's dogs, Duncan and Doughnut, jumped down from the porch and raced after them.

"Darn!" Said Grandma. "I knew we should have kept them in their carrying cases. I'm going to have to go after them."

"Leave them be," said Grandpa. "They'll come in when they're hungry. I told you we should have left them home."

John shook his head. His grandparents were always arguing about the cats. Grandma liked to take them everywhere and Grandpa liked to leave them home.

As soon as they got out of the car, Grandma and Grandpa gave John and Lisa big hugs. "Hope

you aren't having any more encounters with ghosts," said Grandma. "Your mother told me she was worried when you first moved in. She said you were complaining about some ghost in your bedroom."

"It was nothing," said John.

For a minute, he thought of telling his grandmother about the Hessian ghost. But then he changed his mind. It was better not to include any grown-ups in their secret. Even his grandmother might say his imagination was getting the best of him.

During their visit, Grandma and Grandpa took John and Lisa to *The Nutcracker* in New York City. They gave them a new sled for Christmas to use on the big hill near the house. And they took John to a classical concert at Princeton University. But when New Year's came, they had to drive back to Vermont.

After they left, John and Lisa sat in front of the fireplace in the living room, working on a puzzle of a Revolutionary War battle scene that their grandparents had given them. It showed George Washington wintering at Valley Forge after the

Battle of Princeton. Grandma and Grandpa thought that the children would be interested in such a scene, now that they lived in a historic house.

As John fit two pieces of Washington's sword together, he said, "Don't forget, January second is the day after tomorrow. That's the night we'll stay up. Are you ready to meet our ghost?"

"I'm ready," said Lisa. "Although I sometimes wish you hadn't dragged me into this."

"Why? It's all I can think about," said John.

"I know."

"Will you be able to stay awake?"

"I'm a little worried about that. I'm not good at staying up late."

"We can play Monopoly. And I'll also bring my chess set downstairs."

"That will help," said Lisa. "I just hope that when the time comes, I can really go through with this plan of yours."

John crossed his fingers. He hoped he could, too.

CHAPTER TEN

A Meeting with a Hessian Soldier

On the night of January 2, John rolled over and looked at his clock. It was nine-thirty. His parents wouldn't go to sleep for at least an hour. He switched on his light and opened his book, *The Fighting Ground.* It took place during the American Revolution. Even though the story was interesting, John had to struggle to stay awake. He got out of bed and tiptoed around his rug several times to keep from falling asleep. He waited until Mom and Dad came upstairs. When the house was finally quiet, John snuck down the hall to Lisa's room. He opened the door and found her nestled in her blankets, sleeping deeply.

John nudged her several times before she opened her eyes.

"Come on," he said. "We have an appointment with a ghost."

She groaned and turned over. "Tell me what happens in the morning."

"No!" said John. "We made a deal." Lisa didn't budge. John poked her until she rubbed her eyes and sat up.

"Okay, okay, I'm coming," she said. "I have to put on a sweater and some warm socks. I bet it's freezing downstairs."

When Lisa had changed, John took her hand. Together, they tiptoed down the back steps to the kitchen. The stove light was on. They could make out the outlines of the fireplace, table, and chairs. Boomerang was curled up in the rocking chair. Duncan and Doughnut stood up from their sleeping spot by the fireplace and came over. They wagged their tails in hopes that the children would take them for a walk.

"Shhh," hissed John. "Lie down."

Lisa picked up Boomerang and sat down in the rocker.

"It's really cold," she murmured.

John walked over to the kitchen table and opened the Monopoly game.

"Okay," he said. "Which piece do you want?"

"I guess the little Scottie dog. He usually brings me luck."

"I'll be the shoe," said John. "And the banker."

He counted out the money and gave Lisa her share.

They sat at the kitchen table and played for a long time. Lisa bought Park Place and Boardwalk and built four houses on both.

"You're a creep," said John. "If I land there, I'll be wiped out."

Suddenly, Duncan began to growl, a low growl that rolled slowly out of his throat. His fur raised up on his back like little knives. Doughnut stood up, baring his teeth. Both dogs faced the back door. Then, crouching down, their bellies touching the floor, they moved slowly on their haunches toward the door.

John's heart beat wildly as he saw a black boot come right through the wood and into the kitchen. Boomerang leapt from Lisa's lap and sped across the floor, diving behind the stove.

A figure was taking shape in the back of the kitchen. He was a Hessian soldier, all right. He looked about Dad's age. He was wearing a badly torn green coat with red cuffs. Blood dripped from an open wound in his chest, staining the dirty green vest and white shirt he wore underneath. His trousers were the color of mustard and they, too, were torn and dirty above his tall leather boots. The soldier carried a sword with a brass handle, and on his head he wore a three-cornered black hat. He had a bushy black mustache that stretched across the bottom of his face and curled up at the corners. The ghost's eyes had a faraway look in them. It took him a while to focus on the children. He slowly took off his hat and held it under his arm. Then he started to walk toward them!

CHAPTER ELEVEN

The Ghost's Problem

JOHN tried not to scream as the ghost moved closer. The hair lifted up from his scalp and his body felt frozen with goose bumps. It was all he could do to keep his sister from crying out as she grabbed his arm. John would have run, but the ghost stopped a few feet away from them. A smile played around the corners of his mouth and his mustache twitched up in a friendly manner.

"*Eich*, my friends," he said. His voice seemed as if it were coming from the bottom of a deep barrel. It had the rusty sound of not having been used for a long time. "Forgive me. My English is not very good," he said, "even after two hundred years in your country. *Oh Gott.* To you I have wanted to talk since you first moved in and I heard you play the music of Mozart. Mozart's music . . . to hear that sonata . . . it made me long to talk to you . . . but only on the anniversary of the battle can I appear before mortals. And tonight, finally, we meet."

John wanted to say something, but his voice wouldn't work. It was stuck in the back of his throat.

"Do not be frightened," said the Hessian. "I will not harm you. *Ach,* you remind me of my own dear *kinder,* my children, Jared and Mia. They, too, loved music."

"What is your name?" John finally managed to ask.

"Hans Koehler," the ghost answered.

"And have you really been here for two hundred years?"

"*Jah,*" said Hans. "I have haunted this place since the great battle when we lost so many men. . . . And when I heard your music, I thought maybe, after so much time, I could take a chance with you. I hope you can help me find my peace."

John took a deep breath to steady his trembling, not so much from fear as from excitement. Finally, he would hear the ghost's story.

"How can we help you?" he asked. "What problem is keeping you here?"

"My horse, Falada . . ." the ghost said. "I miss her so. But it's a long story. *Das ist eine lange Geschichte.*"

"What do you mean?" asked Lisa. All at once, concern rather than fear showed on her face. "What happened to your horse?" She let go of John's arm and leaned forward.

"*Eich,* let me explain," said the ghost. "For more than two hundred years I have tried to be with her. Ever since losing her . . . but let me go back. I was in Trenton with Colonel Rall's British regiment. He was such a . . .oh, what a stupid man. He was more interested in making merry than performing his duty! Forgive me, I should not say that. . . . I was to stay with him for the winter months. But our plans were ruined when General Washington's troops surprised our men at dawn on the day after *Weihnachten,* Christmas. We had stayed up late the night before, enjoying some excellent food and wine. We were sleeping when the Americans arrived early in the morning. They had rowed across the icy Delaware during a violent storm of snow and hail before attacking us. We were amazed at their bravery. . . . When they marched into Trenton, the sound of musket shots was everywhere. It was a terrible shock. I jumped from my window onto the back of my fine horse, Falada. We rode through blowing snow and cannon smoke to Prince Town."

John's heart beat like a drum. This was such an exciting story.

"What happened next?" he asked.

"I met up with the Sixteenth Regiment of Mounted Dragoons in Prince Town," said Hans Koehler. "Days later we were attacked again by Washington and his men. . . . During the Battle of Prince Town, many men on both sides lost their lives. *Es war eine schreckliche Tragödie.* It was a terrible tragedy. And such sadness . . . Falada, my horse, was shot in the leg and fell from beneath me."

Lisa gasped. "Poor thing! Did she survive?"

"Alas, no. She died in the orchard near Thomas Clarke's house," Hans answered. *"Es war ein schönes Pferd,* she was a beautiful horse. We had been together since I came to America. We saw many a battle, she and I. And when she died, I was so sad. But there was no time to mourn. Minutes later, I was wounded by grapeshot. I was carted on a wagon to the barn behind your house, where I died that night. And for two hundred years, I have heard my horse whinnying on the battlefield, longing for me. . . . Her ghost runs there still, but I cannot go to her. We are divided by the road between us. She haunts the property on one side, I on the other. Ghosts can never leave the property where they died without the help of humans. *Ich war so einsam,* I have been so lonely, so discouraged. . . ."

Lisa struggled to hold back tears as she thought about Hans being separated from his horse.

"But what can we do?" she asked.

"On the anniversary of the battle," said Hans, "the ghosts of the men slain on the battlefield rise from the site of their deaths and re-enact the fight. *Das muss man gesehen haben!* It is a sight to see! Falada will be there this year, as always, and I would be, too, were I not trapped on this property. If you could bring Falada to me . . . if I could be with my dear horse again . . . *ich werde endlich Ruhe finden.* I would have peace at last and could leave your property and haunt it no longer."

Lisa shook her head. "Even if we were to go to the battlefield tonight, how would we recognize your horse?"

"That's easy," said Hans. "She's a splendid chestnut, fifteen hands high, with an English saddle and a brass horn that hangs from her side. And she runs like the wind," he added proudly. "If you take Arab . . ."

"Arab!" exclaimed Lisa. "But he's not used to going out at night. And it's so cold, I worry that—"

"Nonsense!" said John. "You know how strong he is. And we'll need his help! Lisa, please! This is important!"

Lisa gnawed on her finger. "You're right," she said finally. "We could ride Arab over to the battlefield, and maybe, since he heard Falada that day we went out riding, well, I guess he could be helpful."

"I promise he will be," said Hans. "I'll be waiting for you." He began to fade. "For you . . . for you . . ." His voice trailed off as he backed toward the kitchen door. Then he turned and disappeared through the wall.

CHAPTER TWELVE

THE BATTLE OF PRINCETON

IT was so cold in the courtyard that John's breath froze as it hit the air. The moon hung like a great, white stone in the sky.

"I sure am glad it's bright out," said Lisa. "It will be easier to find Falada."

"What did you think of Hans Koehler?" asked John.

"He was frightening. But he looked scarier than he acted. He's really quite nice as ghosts go."

John laughed. What did Lisa know about ghosts? He was the one who had done all the research.

"Those Hessians sure had fancy uniforms," said John. "Ms. Griffin said they were excellent fighters, too. They were well trained, not like the American soldiers who had hardly any time to train. The Americans had fewer supplies, too, and often had to walk miles and miles in the cold without any boots or warm clothes. It's amazing they fought as well as they did."

"It must make a difference when you're fighting for something you believe in," said Lisa. "Like independence."

As soon as they'd bridled up Arab and walked him out to the field, John climbed up behind his sister. He hunched down behind her back, glad it shielded him from the wind that cut through his jacket like a dagger.

Moonlight fell eerily on the muddy field, making the snowy patches look like small ghostly footprints. There was no sign of anyone and the night was completely silent. John shivered as he wondered when the battle would begin.

Arab must have sensed they were embarking on an adventure. His ears were alert and his legs frisky. He crossed the fields to the gate that opened onto the road. As they neared the fence, they could hear whinnying in the distance. Then shots rang out and the smell of gun smoke filled the air.

"Oh, my gosh, look!" said Lisa.

John craned his neck. Through the mist that was rising from the field across the road, he could see figures running back and forth. Lisa dismounted and hurriedly led Arab through the gate, to the fence on the edge of the battlefield.

John's breath caught in his throat. From where he sat on top of the horse, he could see hundreds of men fighting beneath the apple trees near the old Thomas Clarke house. The British and Hessians, marked by their fancy uniforms, were using their bayonets to kill as many Americans as they could. Soldiers on horseback were fighting as well. The sound of moaning and yelling filled the night. Blood from both sides splashed across the patchy snow.

Toward the rear of the American column, someone shouted, "The enemy is upon us!" A group of American soldiers turned and retreated to the safety of the barn by Thomas Clarke's house. Some of the British foot soldiers threw their knapsacks on the ground and grabbed their muskets, while mounted British and Hessians galloped ahead to ambush the American column at the orchard's edge. Cannons boomed. A volley of bullets sent soldiers on both sides diving to the ground. The Americans, many of them barefoot and with torn clothing, were having trouble loading their rifles. While some of them paused, a British officer led his men in a bayonet charge that sent American soldiers flying in all directions.

Lisa covered her eyes at the sight of all the blood, but John's eyes were riveted to the scene before him. Just when it looked as if the Americans were going to lose the battle, a tall, broad-shouldered figure flashing a sword came over the crest of the hill. He rode back and forth in front of the men on a magnificent white horse. "Victory or death!" he shouted.

"Wow!" cried John. "That's George Washington!"

Meanwhile, the wounded were being carried off the field to the Thomas Clarke house and barn. Some were slung onto wagons and others were dropped on the field out of the range of cannon fire. A few of the injured men were laughing giddily, chilling John to the bone.

Suddenly, a huge, riderless chestnut horse raced across the field in front of the children, a horn dangling from its saddle.

"Falada!" shouted John.

"I'm sure it's her!" shouted Lisa. She mounted Arab, sliding in front of John. She grabbed the reins and urged the horse forward. He reared up, then galloped onto the battlefield. John squeezed Lisa around the waist, desperately hanging on. In front of them, Falada's hooves thundered across the field, the mist swirling around her. She circled a group of Americans who were firing on the red-coated British. Their swords flashed in the moonlight.

John could barely keep his balance as Arab overtook Falada, then headed back to the fence, jumping it and racing down the road toward Lawrenceville. Lisa clutched Arab's mane even more tightly.

"Hang on!" she screamed back to John.

"I'm trying to!" he gasped.

"We'll make it," shouted Lisa.

"I hope so!" yelled John.

Holding onto his sister for dear life and gripping Arab as hard as he could with his knees, John turned and looked over his shoulder. Falada was running along the inside of the fence behind them, her sides heaving in and out, froth dripping from her mouth, her breath smudging the cold night air. At last, the horses slowed enough for John to reach over and grab Falada's reins. When the horses finally stopped, Lisa took the reins of Hans's horse from John. Side by side, the horses passed through the gate and across the road to the Perkins' property. Hans Koehler was waiting on a hill, silhouetted tall and proud against the moonlit sky. Lisa let go of Falada's reins. The magnificent chestnut horse whinnied as she trotted toward her old master. Hans grabbed her saddle and mounted atop her broad back. He smiled, his mustache tipping up toward his ears.

"Thank you, my friends. *Vielen dank*," he said. "I can finally go. You have no idea how much this means to me, after all these years of waiting. I go in peace, and may peace be always with you. *Friede sei mit euch.*"

As Falada reared up on her hind legs, framing both horse and rider against the pale moonlight, Hans pulled off his hat and swept it in a high arc against the sky. Frozen for an instant in space, both soldier and horse then turned and bounded over the hill, ghostly partners melting into the swirling fog. It was a scene the children would never forget.

John was speechless as he watched them go. The sound of cannon fire still boomed in the distance. Death cries pierced the night air.

John could see men in red uniforms running down Mercer Street toward the brook, with Washington and his men galloping in pursuit. "It's a fine fox chase, my boys!" the general shouted. Cries of victory rang out in the night as more Americans raced toward Prince Town, disappearing in the mist.

The sounds moved off toward the center of town as more men left the battlefield.

"Ms. Griffin told us that the battle took only forty-five minutes. Do you think we should go back to the battlefield and help the wounded?" John asked.

"You've forgotten—they're all ghosts," Lisa said. "Besides, I'd rather live with the memory of what we just saw and the thought that the Americans performed a great feat tonight."

"A feat that led to an American victory," said John. "It's kind of exciting to think that our house played a small role."

"And that our soldier is finally at peace," said Lisa. "Believe it or not, I'm actually going to miss him."

"Me, too," said John. "I can't wait to tell Obadiah the latest. Even his aunt Rose won't believe the story about the battlefield."

Lisa was quiet for a second. Then she said, "I don't see why anyone needs to hear about our ghost. They'd just make fun or insist we were making him up. You shouldn't tell Obadiah one more word about him."

"But he's my best friend."

"I know, but it would kind of spoil it. Hans was *our* ghost and he should be our secret. If we keep sharing the stuff that happened, it won't be special anymore."

John looked up at the moon, shining like a silver coin. For a moment, he thought he heard someone humming. He tipped his head to catch the tune, then heard nothing. Was it Hans humming or had he just *wanted* to hear him? John thought about what Lisa had said. She was right. Hans had come to them for help and they had given it. He *was* their special secret.

"I agree," said John "Let's not tell anyone anything more."

Turning onto the path that led to the barn, they both smiled, happy to know that two ghosts were finally at peace.

THE STORY
BEHIND THE STORY

THE American War of Independence was fought by the American colonists against Great Britain from 1775 to 1783. Stretching along the eastern seaboard, the original colonies consisted of Massachusetts, Rhode Island, Connecticut, New York, Pennsylvania, New Jersey, Delaware, Maryland, New Hampshire, Virginia, North Carolina, South Carolina, and Georgia. They were settled by English, Dutch, Scottish, and other immigrants, who left their homes on the far side of the Atlantic to begin a new life in North America. The land in the New World belonged to Great Britain, which had won it after a nine-year war with France (the French and Indian War, 1754–63).

Although Britain had emerged the winner, its treasury was drained after so many years of fighting. To raise money to pay its debts, the British Parliament ordered the American colonists to pay a series of stiff taxes on tea and other goods. This enraged the colonists, who had no voice in the British Parliament. Tension between England and the colonists continued to build, finally resulting in rebellion. On April 19, 1775, a "shot heard round the world" was fired by an American on a group of seven hundred British soldiers in Concord, Massachusetts, marking the beginning of the American Revolution.

On June 15, 1775, George Washington was appointed general and commander in chief of the American army. The army, made up mainly of farmers, was ill equipped and poorly trained compared to the British army. In addition, the British hired thousands of Hessian soldiers,

German mercenaries from the province of Hesse, who were willing to fight for pay. In the Declaration of Independence, King George III of England was accused of "transporting large Armies of foreign Mercenaries to compleat the works of death, desolation and tyranny, already begun with circumstances of Cruelty and perfidy scarcely paralleled in the most barbarous ages, and totally unworthy of the Head of a civilized nation."

The Hessian mercenaries were trained to take meticulous care of their arms, clothes, and weapons. Strict rules regulated how the recruits were to walk, stand, exercise, and even dress. In the evening, every soldier curled up his hair in papers, then powdered and brushed it before going on duty in the morning. The men stiffened their mustaches with black wax and shined their brass helmets until they glistened. Every soldier was given a comb, brush, mirror, wax for his shoes and whiskers, a piece of buff leather, a wooden polisher, a screwdriver, a set of gaiter buttons, and a hook for buttoning his gaiters, which were cloth or leather ankle coverings.

Britain paid half a million dollars for every ten thousand Hessians. If a soldier was killed, his death would cost Britain an additional thirty-five dollars, and if a soldier was wounded, the additional cost would be twelve dollars. The American government offered land and two cows to any Hessian who deserted. Of the thirty thousand who came to America, approximately twelve thousand were killed or else settled in the New World.

Hans Koehler in *The Battlefield Ghost* was a *Jaeger* (or *Jäger),* which means "hunter" in German. The *Jaeger* troops were recruited from among the huntsmen and foresters of the German state. Their main function was to support the infantry or foot soldiers by using their muskets or rifles against American units before the infantry advanced to fight them. By 1777, there were five foot companies and one mounted company of Jaegers in North America.

Colonel Johann Gottlieb Rall, mentioned in connection with the Battle of Trenton, was a Hessian grenadier. Usually taller than the other soldiers, the grenadiers generally were considered more intelligent. Their muskets were heavy flintlock firearms, and they also carried short swords and bayonets. They were specially trained to use the bayonets on the end of their muskets, and for this reason, much American blood was shed in the Battle of Princeton.

The Battle of Princeton, fought on January 3, 1777 — and the Battle of Trenton, fought one week previously, on December 26, 1776 — changed the course of the war. Although there was an early American victory at Fort Ticonderoga, New York (May 10, 1775), the Americans afterwards suffered a series of defeats. One of Washington's men, Thomas Paine, also the author of a famous pamphlet, *Common Sense,* that urged American independence, wrote in December, 1776, "These are the times that try men's souls. . . . Tyranny, like Hell, is not easily conquered."

If it were not for Washington's brilliant strategy to cross the Delaware in the middle of the night in order to surprise the enemy at dawn — before the Battle of Trenton and again before the Battle of Princeton — the British might have won the war. The weather conditions were terrible — heavy snow and hail; choppy, icy waters; bitter northeastern winds; and below-freezing temperatures. The boats were small and not designed for the heavy cannons and other artillery that the Americans had to transport. Once across the river, the men had to walk in the pitch black on highways covered with snow. Poorly clothed, hungry, and exhausted, some of the men did not even have boots or shoes. Their feet bled from the sharp, icy edges of the snow.

Had Colonel Rall acted more responsibly, the Americans might have fared less well in Trenton. But the colonel had a reputation for enjoying himself rather than tending to his troops. Described by an Englishman as "noisy, but not sullen, unacquainted with the language, and a drunkard," Rall had stayed up late on Christmas night, playing cards and feasting extravagantly. His men had also relaxed, celebrating the holiday with rum and extra food rations. Most were still in bed on the morning of December 26th, when Washington's troops attacked. Washington took one thousand prisoners and suffered only six wounded, including a future president of the United States, James Monroe.

About Washington's conduct in both battles, a Prussian writer, Dietrich Heinrich von Bulow, known for his writings on military tactics, wrote that the Battle of Trenton was "one of the best planned and most ably executed" military battles of the century. "It was, however, excelled by the

Princeton offensive, and both operations are sufficient to elevate a general to the temple of immortality."

Much has been written about the behavior of the British and American armies. In general, the Americans were considered kinder than the enemy. "You are safe enough, we are after live men," they assured those wounded enemy soldiers who begged for mercy, even sharing their food if they were lucky enough to have any. The wounded in the Battle of Princeton were either cared for immediately at Thomas Clarke's house or at other houses in the area, or carried by wagon into Princeton. It is possible that the house known as The Barracks in Princeton, New Jersey, was used to house wounded Hessians. To this day, there is a legend that on Christmas Eve, a Hessian ghost ascends the chimney of the fireplace in the old kitchen. It is the house in which I grew up and still live, and although in the book I changed the exact location of the house and the date of the ghost's appearance, this is the legend that inspired me to write *The Battlefield Ghost*.

Made in the USA
San Bernardino, CA
28 September 2016